A FALCON GUIDE®

BASIC ESSENTIA

BASIC ✳ ESSENTIALS®
SEA KAYAKING

THIRD EDITION

J. MICHAEL WYATT

REVISED BY ROGER SCHUMANN

FALCONGUIDE®

GUILFORD, CONNECTICUT
HELENA, MONTANA
AN IMPRINT OF THE GLOBE PEQUOT PRESS

A FALCON GUIDE®

Text and page design by Casey Shain
Illustrations on pages 3, 34, and 51 by Diane Blasius, others by Denise Harris
Photos on pages 25, 26, and 31 courtesy of Roger Schumann

Library of Congress Cataloging-in-Publication Data

Wyatt, Mike, 1953-
 Basic essentials. Sea kayaking / J. Michael Wyatt; revised by Roger Schumann. — 3rd ed.
  p. cm. — (A Falcon Guide) (Basic essentials series)
 Includes bibliographical references (p.) and index.
 ISBN 0-7627-3832-4
  1. Sea kayaking. I. Title: Sea kayaking. II. Schumann, Roger. III. Title. IV. Series.

GV788.5.W93 2005
797.122'4—dc22   2005046023

Manufactured in the United States of America
Third Edition/First Printing

Contents

Help Us Keep This Guide Up to Date

Every effort has been made by the authors and editors to make this guide as accurate and useful as possible. However, many things can change after a guide is published—new products and information become available, regulations change, techniques evolve, etc.

We would love to hear from you concerning your experience with this guide and how you feel it could be improved and be kept up to date. While we may not be able to respond to all comments and suggestions, we'll take them to heart and we'll also make certain to share them with the authors. Please send your comments and suggestions to the following address:

The Globe Pequot Press
Reader Response/Editorial Department
P.O. Box 480
Guilford, CT 06437

Or you may e-mail us at:

editorial@GlobePequot.com

Thanks for your input, and happy travels!

The Boat

What Is a Sea Kayak?

For many paddlers, a *kayak* is much more than just a boat: It is their exercise machine, a way to find peace in nature, and the ultimate off-road adventure vehicle. Less lyrically, a kayak is a narrow boat with an open area near the middle where the paddler sits. Propulsion and steering are provided by a two-bladed paddle. If a kayak carries one person, it's called a single or sometimes a K-1. If it carries two people, it's known variously as a double, tandem, or K-2.

Originally adapted to match regional conditions and paddling styles, kayak designs vary as widely as do the environments for which they were intended. Although there's some crossover and hybridization, modern-day kayaks are typically designed with the following uses in mind: day or overnight touring, racing, ocean surfing, and running white-water rivers. General touring kayaks are the focus of this book, with an emphasis on closed-deck sea kayaks.

Types of Sea Kayaks

Touring Kayaks

Designed to be stable, comfortable, and easy to paddle at cruising speeds, typical *touring kayaks* are built to carry the loads necessary to support a paddler on a long trip. These boats average 15 to 18 feet in length with a beam of 23 to 26 inches. Touring kayaks are suited to a range of skill levels and allow for a number of uses, including photography, bird-watching, and fishing, in addition to touring.

Narrower performance models with beams in the 20-inch range can be fast and exciting to paddle, but they are less stable and require a higher level of skill to operate. Although sleek and efficient, they may not be the best choice for loading up with camping gear and heading out on a long trip because of their reduced storage capacity.

At the short end of the touring-kayak spectrum are boats in the 13- to 15-foot range. Quick and maneuverable, they can be a lot of fun on day trips, but they tend to lack the speed and carrying capacity to be the boat of choice for multiday expeditions; if packed carefully, they're fine for overnights and shorter trips. Where they really shine, however, is on day trips along the open coast, where more advanced paddlers enjoy their quickness for surfing waves and playing in ocean rock gardens.

Recreational Kayaks

The new style of *recreational kayaks,* or "rec boats," is an inexpensive option for those planning short nearshore trips in protected waters such as ponds, sloughs, or slow-moving rivers. Typically short (9 to 15 feet), wide (25 to 30 inches), and stable, with relatively large and open cockpits, these boats are easy on beginners and their pocketbooks. Generally they are ill suited to actual touring, however, because their broad hulls tend to be slow and inefficient. Most also have no bulkheads and little or no flotation, so not only is there little room for gear, but they are not particularly seaworthy, either. The open-water rescues described later in the book are extremely difficult or impossible to perform on capsized rec boats due to the large amount of water they tend to take on. Some swamped compacts float so low in the water, in fact, that the only way to drain them is to drag the "submarined" kayak to shore.

Open-Deck Kayaks

Of the many open-deck or "sit-on-top" kayaks available, plastic *day-touring models* have become quite popular, especially in warm-water environments. Typically ranging from 10 to 15 feet long and 25 to 30 inches or more in width, these boats have open, self-bailing cockpits that are quite user-friendly for beginners; they also require less specific rescue skills than closed-deck kayaks do. Their stable, beamy hulls, however, are less efficient than sleeker sea kayaks, especially in wind, and most lack the stowage to accommodate overnight camping gear. Some models include scuba tank storage compartments, making them particularly useful for divers.

Surf skis, which began as ocean rescue craft in Australia and South Africa, are another type of open-deck kayak. These sleek, fast, and sexy boats are popular for racing, fitness paddling, and surfing. Racing surf skis average 19 feet long with a beam of only 17 inches—clearly built for speed, not stability. Recreational models top out with a beam of 20 inches, still narrow by conventional touring-kayak standards. Although

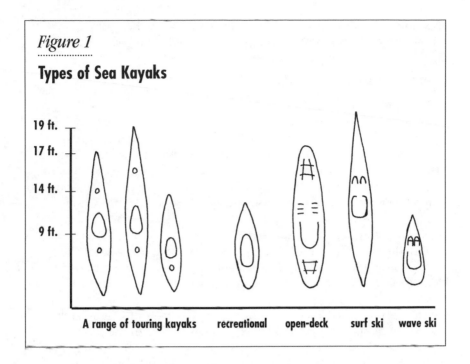

Figure 1

Types of Sea Kayaks

19 ft.
17 ft.
14 ft.
9 ft.

A range of touring kayaks   recreational   open-deck   surf ski   wave ski

fast, efficient, and seaworthy, most surf skis lack storage compartments for touring.

    Wave skis are the squat cousins of surf skis. Averaging just 6 to 9 feet in length, they look like a cross between a kayak and a surfboard. The majority are performance play boats designed specifically for surfing ocean waves, so they have no storage and are not suited for touring. Other surf and specialty kayaks include short, white-water river kayaks that are sometimes used to surf ocean waves; high-performance surf kayaks designed specifically for surfing; and a variety of racing kayaks.

Materials and Construction

Fiberglass

    Many sea kayaks are made of a molded fiberglass-and-resin composite. This combination of materials produces a lightweight, strong, and durable boat for a reasonable price. General touring sea kayaks typically weigh between 50 to 60 pounds for a single and 80 to 90 pounds for a double. The widest range of touring designs are available in fiberglass, and the performance characteristics of their stiff, smooth, lightweight hulls are hard to beat. On the downside they cost much more than plastic kayaks, and they are not as indestructible. If you do crack a hull on a rock, however, they are fairly easy to repair.

Kevlar and Carbon Fiber

Many manufacturers offer Kevlar or carbon-fiber versions of fiberglass models. The use of these strong, high-tech materials allows boatbuilders to trim 5 to 10 pounds or more off the weight of a typical fiberglass model. This reduction in weight increases performance slightly. They are also easier to carry and put onto a car, which can be especially attractive to those who sometimes paddle alone. Whether or not this justifies the several hundred dollars' extra cost, however, is something to consider.

Plastic

Introduced in the early 1980s, molded polyethylene sea kayaks have steadily grown in popularity. Heavier, but less expensive and more rugged than their fiberglass or folding counterparts, plastic boats are excellent entry-level sea kayaks.

The great expense involved in producing the molds has limited the designs of plastic sea kayaks to those that will appeal to the largest potential markets. As a result plastic sea kayaks aren't offered in as many different designs and levels of performance as can be found in fiberglass boats. However, each year new models are introduced, and there are now many models designed specifically for more advanced paddlers.

Wood

Kayaks constructed of wood are lighter than plastic, at least as strong as fiberglass, and can be works of art more beautiful than either. Designs are fairly limited (unless you can create your own) in the kits and books currently available. The cost of a kit or of the required materials is generally less than that of ready-made kayaks, but space, time, and tools will factor into your total outlay. Maintaining wooden kayaks' finish is key to preserving their beauty and durability.

Skin

Although not widespread, interest in the art of re-creating traditional skin designs is growing. Instead of reproducing the Aleut *baidarkas* or Greenland kayak designs out of bones or real seal skins, though, builders are turning to aluminum or wooden frames covered with "skins" of sturdy nylon or canvas, which are then given a waterproof coating. Some of these kayaks are being sold custom built; others are built from kits. Skin boats cost about the same but can be 10 to 20 pounds lighter than fiberglass boats. Further, depending on the skin and its maintenance, a skin boat can be more durable and forgiving.

Folding

Folding boats have long been the mainstay of paddlers with a wanderlust. They have amply proved their toughness and seaworthiness on expeditions throughout the world, including the first transatlantic crossing by kayak, more than sixty years ago.

Of all modern kayaks, folding models are the most reminiscent of aboriginal wood-and-skin craft. They are built of a waterproof fabric skin stretched over a rigid frame of wood or tubular aluminum. The boats are typically much beamier than hardshell kayaks, and the cockpits are quite large. A few manufacturers, however, now offer sleeker models that rival hardshells in width and performance.

Folding boats range in weight from 30 pounds for a single to 90 pounds for a double. A single kayak will pack into a bag the size of a large suitcase, but such portability comes at a price: Folding boats are among the most expensive sea-touring kayaks.

Inflatable

Inflatable kayaks are increasing in acceptance and popularity, especially in the warm waters of the tropical Pacific, where their transportability, seaworthiness, and ability to bounce through hard landings are important features. Open and beamy, they are generally much less efficient than hardshells. Inflatables are typically divided into several air compartments: three major ones located in each side and the bottom, and smaller ones located in the bow, stern, and seats. The boats gain their rigidity from the 2 to 4 pounds per square inch of air pressure that inflates them. Weights range from 20 to 50 pounds, and prices range from under $200 to more than $1,000.

Kayak Features

Rudders

A *rudder* is a flat-bladed steering apparatus controlled by a pair of foot pedals. Two cables, one for each pedal, run from the pedals to the rudder and allow you to rotate the blade right and left on a fixed point set in the stern of the kayak. The rudder is also hinged to lift up and slip over seaweed and other obstructions while the boat is moving forward in the water. A line is used to cock the rudder up and out of the way during transport, launching, and landing, and while backing over obstructions.

Rudders, although available as an option on nearly every boat made today, have been a subject of dispute among sea-kayaking experts for years. Most either love them or hate them. Those who favor rudders cite improved paddling efficiency and the ease of hands-free maneuverability. Paddling purists point to rudders as another piece of equipment that can fail and as a device that lessens the paddler's reliance on basic paddling skills. And the flex or stretch of rudder cables makes for less firm support from the foot braces.

Over the years improved designs, incorporating tougher materials and construction, have increased the dependability of rudders. In a crosswind a rudder allows you to maintain a course with a minimum of wasted energy spent in corrective strokes, enabling you to devote your energies to propulsion rather than position.

A rudder is especially handy to anyone bird-watching, taking photographs, or fishing from a kayak. As a first-time boat buyer, if you purchase a kayak with a rudder, you'll have an opportunity to try it both ways. If you don't like it, you can always leave it cocked out of the water.

Hatches

Hatches allow easy access through the deck to gear stored inside the boat: Even bulky items such as camera cases and sleeping bags can be easily stowed and retrieved. Some feel that hatches invite disaster by compromising the waterproof integrity and strength of a solid deck, but as in the case of rudders, this objection has largely been overcome by improved designs.

Generally, smaller hatches are sometimes more watertight and dependable than larger models but can make stowing or accessing gear more difficult. Look for secure and easy-to-operate closures and hatch designs that offer a positive seal through the use of a durable gasket. Never assume that a hatch is waterproof.

Bulkheads

Bulkheads are watertight walls that divide the sections of a hardshell kayak's interior into compartments. They provide discrete areas for stowing gear and, much like the watertight compartments on larger boats, offer some measure of improved safety by providing buoyancy in case of a capsize.

Don't assume that a bulkhead alone will keep your unprotected gear dry. Some designs may not provide enough buoyancy to keep your boat afloat in the event of a capsize. To be on the safe side, some paddlers add flotation in the form of dry bags or inflatable float bags.

Figure 2

The Parts of a Closed-Deck Touring Sea Kayak

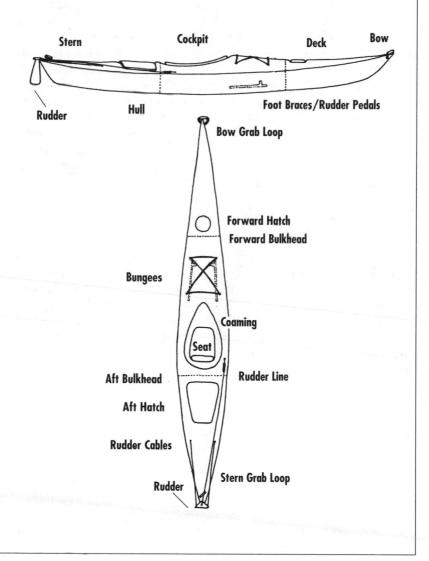

Bulkheads are usually made of fiberglass-resin sheet glassed in place, or rigid closed-cell foam secured with a flexible adhesive. You'll usually find bulkheads aft of the seat and forward of the foot braces.

Seats

Of all the features of a kayak, the seat is probably the single most troublesome—correct seat designs are as varied as the bottoms and backs they're supposed to fit. Fortunately the seat is also the easiest feature to replace or adapt to your individual needs. Ideally a kayak seat should provide a low center of gravity while lifting you enough to create a leg position that's comfortable for long periods of time. The seat back should provide adequate lumbar support without interfering with motion. The overall feel should be comfortable, with a secure feel for the boat.

If you find that the seat needs to be adapted to your contours, sections of closed-cell foam like that found in backpacking sleeping pads can usually be glued in place with a waterproof adhesive or attached with duct tape. Some kayakers sit on inflatable backpacking cushions; one camp mattress manufacturer even makes an inflatable seat designed specifically for use in sea kayaks. Replacing hard seat backs with padded back bands is also becoming more common.

Selecting a Kayak

When to Buy

If you're a novice paddler, you should gain as much experience as possible through classes and on-the-water time in rentals before deciding to purchase a boat. Your ability to judge the feel of a kayak will be largely dependent on your experience and skill level. As your skills and confidence increase, so will your ability to evaluate the qualities of a boat's performance. Remember that the best choice is your choice, but you must be sure that you're making an informed decision.

Which Model?

The first question that any prospective boat buyer should consider is: "What will I *really* use the boat for?" Try to answer this question as honestly as possible. In the highly subjective world of kayak design, each of the many boats available defines the needs of the sea kayaker a little differently. If you'll be using the boat exclusively for day trips or fitness paddling, space for gear is not an issue. But if you plan to go on long-distance tours, a high-volume boat becomes a necessity. If you're an avid photographer or angler, stability is important. If most of your trips will involve travel by air, or if you lack storage for a hardshell boat, an inflatable or folding boat should be considered. If you're single, a single is your best choice, but if you'll be paddling with your partner or children, you might consider a double.

The answer to this question of model, then, depends largely on your location, your interests, and your skill level. One of the common errors of first-time boat buyers is to choose the type of boat suited to their long-term goals but not their present needs. Don't get a folding boat now because you plan to visit Crete someday. Don't get a narrow and demanding sport boat if it's unlikely that you'll have the time or the interest to develop the paddling skills it requires.

At the Store

After you've defined how you'll use your boat, it's time to try a few on. To further narrow the field, visit your dealer's sales floor. Select the boats that meet your basic needs. Take an inventory of features and look at materials, workmanship, and prices.

Now climb in and get a feel for the fit. Is the cockpit large or small enough to accommodate you comfortably? Is there adequate foot room? Will the deck height and seat position allow adequate elbow clearance? Can you firmly brace your knees? Does the seat feel snug and supportive? If the boat feels right, rent one.

On the Water

Until you've had a chance to be in the boat for at least a few hours, you have no way of knowing if its fit and feel are to your liking. Your dealer should have a selection of showroom models available for rental. To try out a wide variety in a short time, attend a dealer's "demo day," where many models are on the beach for trial.

Don't get too hung up on finding the "perfect kayak": Any decision regarding a boat purchase will involve compromise. No one kayak design can incorporate all the features you desire, but with a little time and patience, you can find a boat with the combination of features best suited to your needs.

Gear

Paddle

The paddle is your propulsion, steering, and stabilizer. You'll have it in your hands nearly all the time you're in your boat. And in the course of even a brief trip, you'll move the paddle through countless strokes. Next to your kayak, a paddle is the most important and personal piece of gear you'll purchase.

Materials

Sea-touring paddles are available in a wide variety of materials in a number of combinations, which determine the paddle's strength, weight, durability, and cost. The heaviest and least-expensive paddles have metal shafts and plastic blades. Fiberglass or wood is common for midweight, midprice paddles; wooden paddles tend to be as light as or lighter than fiberglass, but not as durable. Paddles made from Kevlar, graphite, or carbon fiber are typically the lightest, but they also tend to be less durable and quite expensive.

Weight

The most expensive paddles—those that require particular attention during production and incorporate such space-age materials as graphite— are nearly always also the lightest in weight. These paddles can weigh well under 2 pounds, while the heaviest tip the scales at more than 3 pounds. This weight range of little more than a pound may at first seem inconsequential and little justification for a price increase of as much as 100 percent or more, but after tens of thousands of paddle strokes during a long trip—considering that the average paddler takes around 1,000 strokes per mile—even a few ounces can begin to count very heavily. So don't scrimp: Money spent on a decent paddle will seem well worth it after a long day on the water. The lightest paddles are great for long-distance touring on flat water, but you may want something a little sturdier for more challenging conditions or skills practice.

Length

There is no formula for selecting the correct length of paddle. Beyond a few basic considerations, it's a matter of personal preference. The most common length for a general touring paddle is between 7 and 8 feet (210 and 240 cm). The best paddle for you is one suited to your size and strength and the size and handling of your boat. Remember that beamier boats often require longer paddles, and narrow boats often require shorter paddles. Longer paddles put more leverage into each stroke but require more effort. Shorter paddles require less leverage and allow for a faster cadence and smoother acceleration. In recent years there has been a definite trend toward shorter paddles. Most modern-day kayak racers use paddles of 220 cm or less with a high-cadence, vertical stroke technique—which also works well for recreational paddlers in more demanding conditions.

Blade Shapes

Wider blades (6 to 8 inches or more) supply greater resistance and are considered more powerful for acceleration than narrow blades, but the added width can cause more strain on wrist, arm, and shoulder tendons. So-called touring designs, such as traditional Aleut- and Greenland-style paddles, have long, narrow blades (typically less than 5 inches). These paddles tend to have slower acceleration and less overall power, but they are less fatiguing, especially on longer trips in loaded kayaks.

Asymmetric blades, common on many sea-kayak paddles, have less blade surface on the portion of the blade below the line of the shaft. As the blade enters and moves through the water at an angle, torque is reduced by exposing each half of the blade face to equal amounts of pressure. This balances the load along the centerline of the blade face, reducing the paddle's tendency to twist in the water and improving paddling efficiency.

Most modern paddle blades are both *dihedral* and *spooned* slightly. The former reduces flutter (rapid side-to-side twisting motion) and sideways slippage by encouraging the water to flow off both halves of the blade face evenly; the latter provides more power by holding the water. Racers use an extreme design called a *wing* with a pronounced scoop to its blade; this provides a more positive "bite" on the water during a forward stroke but can take some getting used to, especially with other strokes.

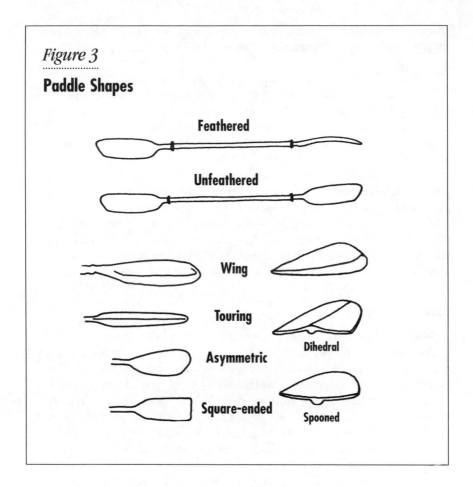

Figure 3

Paddle Shapes

Feathered

Unfeathered

Wing

Touring

Dihedral

Asymmetric

Square-ended

Spooned

Feathered or Unfeathered?

A *feathered* paddle has blades rotated at an angle on the axis of the shaft. An *unfeathered* paddle has its blades on the same plane.

There is endless debate about the advantages and disadvantages of feathered and unfeathered paddles, and any paddler you ask will probably have a strong opinion. Feathered blades offer less resistance to a headwind, while unfeathered blades are best in a wind from the side. Unfeathered blades also require less wrist and forearm motion and are less likely to cause tendonitis. Each type works well under different circumstances and neither is best for all conditions. If you're a novice paddler, your best bet is not to enter the fray—try both by using a two-piece breakdown paddle that adjusts to either feathered or unfeathered position and stick with the one that feels best to you.

Accessories

Spray Skirt

The *spray skirt* is a water-resistant barrier that seals around your abdomen and the boat's coaming to keep water from entering the boat through the cockpit.

Spray skirts are made out of neoprene wet-suit material or coated nylon fabric. The rubber material is flexible; it stretches taut over the coaming and gives a snug fit around your waist, forming a positive seal and a smooth surface that sheds water. Coated nylon provides greater ventilation and a more comfortable fit. It won't stretch, so it's not as snug and will tend to pool water. Some models use both materials—neoprene to stretch over the coaming and nylon fabric around your abdomen— taking advantage of the best qualities of each and making a nice compromise. Snug-fitting all-neoprene skirts work best for practicing kayak rolls or paddling in rough water or surf.

Life Vest or PFD

A life vest or, more correctly, PFD (personal flotation device) is an essential part of every kayaker's outfit. PFDs required for sea touring are certified by the U.S. Coast Guard as Type III (marked on the label inside the vest). They are constructed of a nylon shell filled with vertical sections of closed-cell foam. PFDs intended for general boating are not appropriate for kayaking; their long waists interfere with the spray skirt. PFDs intended for kayaking are cut like a high vest.

The role of a PFD is simple: In case of a capsize, it enables you to float at the surface without expending precious energy. To do this, the vest must be in the right place at the right time—on you when you go into the water. A comfortable fit is very important. Look for a style that's fairly snug but will allow adequate layers of clothing for the conditions you'll typically encounter while paddling. The fit around your arms should allow ample room for movement, and PFDs with pockets provide handy access to items such as sunscreen, snack bars, or safety flares.

Dry Bags

Waterproof dry bags are available in both coated nylon and PVC materials. Roll-down closures are the easiest to use and provide the most dependable seals. PVC bags are generally more durable than nylon and are widely available in a variety of sizes and weights.

When purchasing waterproof PVC gear bags, look for quality materials. The strength of PVC bags is in the thread—the vinyl only provides the seal. The fiber scrim of nylon or polyester gives a bag its tensile strength and puncture resistance. Less expensive PVC fabrics have a lower thread count, indicated by the larger gaps in the screenlike pattern of the underlying threads. PVC bags have two sides—a textured scrim side and a smooth face side. To check thread count, examine the scrim side.

The material's thickness, combined with denier and thread count, is the best indication of the fabric's overall ability to withstand abrasion, punctures, cutting, and tearing. Heavier, stiffer materials do not fold as tightly and will not form as reliable a seal in a standard roll-down closure as will a lighter-weight fabric. Weight works against the "hand" of the material—generally, the heavier the material, the stiffer its feel—so you must usually compromise between the bag's watertightness and its durability.

Flotation

Flotation is essential to safety in the event of a capsize. On a long trip flotation can be provided by a boatload of gear stowed in dry bags. For shorter trips, float bags are the answer. These contoured nylon or plastic inflatable bags fit into the boat's bow and stern.

Paddlefloat Self-Rescue Device

This is an essential piece of safety gear with any closed-cockpit kayak—as long as you have training on how to use it and practice regularly. Lack of paddlefloat or inability to perform a self-rescue is a common theme in kayak accident reports. For a description of the device and its use, see Paddlefloat Self-Rescue in Chapter 4.

Spare Paddle

Like a spare tire in a car, a spare paddle should be taken on every trip for use if the primary paddle breaks or gets lost. In a group of kayakers, one spare is generally considered sufficient, as long as the group stays together.

Pumps and Sponges

Small high-volume hand pumps, found at kayaking stores, are necessary for emergency bailing following a capsize. Battery-powered electric pumps are also available but not common.

A large sponge is handy for sopping up the last remnants of water and for general cleaning.

Whistle or Air Horn

A waterproof whistle attached to your PFD or a compact compressed air horn provides a clear, loud, and distinctive means of signaling other members of your party.

Waterproof Flashlight

Not only are flashlights handy if you return late, but a light is actually required by the Coast Guard for paddling after dark.

Towline

A towline—at least 30 feet of ¼-inch line—should be part of every paddler's basic gear.

Emergency Signal Kit

Emergency signals have two purposes: to attract attention and to indicate your location in the event of an emergency that requires rescue or prompt medical attention. Every kayaker should carry a set of emergency signals and be familiar with their most effective use. In case of emergency, they must be easily accessible.

A BASIC KIT COULD CONTAIN:

◆ pack of three "pocket" aerial flares

◆ smoke canister

◆ air horn

◆ signal mirror

A MORE COMPLETE KIT MIGHT ALSO CONTAIN:

◆ VHF radio and/or cell phone

◆ Strobe

◆ Parachute flares

◆ Marker dye

Weather Radio

Handy for day trips and indispensable on long tours, inexpensive pocket weather radios can provide you with current conditions and forecasts from National Oceanic and Atmospheric Administration weather stations.

Clothing

Safety-conscious kayakers use the phrase "dress for immersion" when preparing for a trip. This implies dressing for the temperature of the water, not the air temperature, and you should remember that you can become hypothermic in seventy-degree water. Kayaking is a water sport. To participate fully, anticipate getting wet. Compared to being dry, you can lose body heat five times faster when wet and twenty times faster when immersed. Weigh your chances of a capsize against the cost of not preparing for that event, and consider spray and wind a part of each day on the water. Wear synthetic fabrics designed to insulate even if wet (wool also works this way). Cotton, however, only warms if dry, which is why some outdoor experts say, "cotton kills." So cotton is not recommended unless you'll be paddling in water of around eighty degrees or so.

Layering is a good way to dress for changing conditions on the water. In a kayak your upper body experiences the greatest range of temperatures and conditions. It's exposed to the elements and will lose and gain heat through a variety of mechanisms, from heat loss through convection (wind) to heat gain through work (paddling). You can use your clothing to regulate the temperature and maintain a comfortable range.

Layer One—Vapor Transmission

This is the layer next to your skin, and its role is to lessen evaporative cooling by transmitting moisture to the next layer. Snug-fitting underwear made of nonabsorbent plastic fibers, such as polypropylene or polyester, is your best choice. Look for a lightweight fabric intended for active use.

Layer Two—Insulation

This layer traps and holds air warmed by your body. Pile or fleece is your best choice. Avoid collars, cuffs, or hems made of absorbent knit. In locations where water temperature is less than sixty-five degrees or so, wet suits are recommended. The most popular wet suits for sea touring are 3-mm (⅛-inch) neoprene farmer john style (full body and legs, no sleeves).

Layer Three—Shell

This layer shields you from wind and water. Without it the effectiveness of the two previous layers is greatly reduced. Avoid open cuffs, which allow water to run down your arms as you paddle. There are a number of waterproof shells called paddling jackets or spray jackets designed specifically for sea kayaking that offer features such as neoprene cuff and neck closures, functional hoods, and handy pockets positioned to clear the top of your spray skirt. Dry suits or dry jackets are sometimes used in colder climates. More expensive than wet suits, they offer greater safety and warmth by acting as a waterproof shell with tight rubber seals at the wrists and neck.

Ventilation is important to the functioning of the other layers—you must have a way to effectively vent accumulating heat and moisture. Unfortunately, ventilation sometimes compromises waterproofness, and a paddling jacket that lets air out may also let water in. However, modern "breathable" waterproof fabrics such as PacLite and others, albeit more expensive, are less clammy and more comfortable to paddle in than standard coated-nylon paddling jackets.

In hot summer weather or the tropics, coolness and protection from the sun are your greatest concerns. A long-sleeved cotton shirt paired with quick-drying shorts will work well. The cotton fabric will accumulate salt quickly and develop a greasy feel if it isn't periodically rinsed in fresh water. A light wind shell will provide protection from cool breezes on and off the water, and a pair of light cotton pants will make for comfortable morning and evening beach attire.

Head

If your rain shell doesn't have an adequate hood, a sou' wester-style rain hat works well. Its brim will channel dripping water away from your face and out of your field of vision. Select a size large enough to accommodate a wool or synthetic fleece cap.

For sunny weather a wide-brimmed cotton hat with a chin tie for windy weather will prevent sun from hitting both your face and the back of your neck. A baseball cap protects your face and head while staying on better in the wind (and a cap leash can retain it when it doesn't). On particularly warm days cool your head by dipping the hat in the water before putting it on.

Your head can account for up to one-half of your body's total heat loss. In cold water where there is a chance of a capsize, or when practicing rolls and rescues, adequate head insulation is important to your comfort and safety. Neoprene caps, like those used by white-water boaters, or full neoprene hoods keep you much warmer. Skullcaps that cut wind and don't absorb water are warmer than neoprene when your head is not submerged.

Hands

For cold-weather paddling nothing can beat the warmth and direct hand-to-paddle contact of pogies. These mittlike hand covers are made of neoprene or waterproof nylon, with a liner made of synthetic fleece. The assembled units open to slip over the paddle shaft and secure with Velcro closures. You simply slip your hands inside and grab the paddle shaft. In sunny weather the outer fabric shells of pogies make great sun protection for the backs of your hands—a place very susceptible to sunburn while paddling. Many paddlers, however, prefer the increased mobility of gloves over pogies—neoprene for warmth or lightweight, fingerless spandex types with faux-leather palms (similar to cycling gloves without padding) for sun and blister protection.

Feet

In warm climates sandals or lightweight water shoes that fit securely and will stay in place in the water are your best choice. A recommended type has durable and supportive rubber foot beds, midsoles, and soles, along with nylon webbing straps and plastic snaps.

Cold-water paddlers sometimes prefer waterproof rubber or plastic "farm" boots. Combined with wool socks, they provide a good combination of warmth, comfort, and dryness. Their biggest drawback is bulk—larger sizes often won't fit in the limited space of a kayak and still allow full movement of rudder pedals, and they are difficult to perform rescues in. Another choice is neoprene booties. They provide warmth and, with a durable sole, protection from rocks while wading, but they're uncomfortable to wear for long periods. Many outdoor retailers now carry shoes designed for water sports that have soles made for traction on wet surfaces and uppers made of fast-drying fabrics.

Paddle Techniques

Fitting Your Kayak

Kayakers have a saying: "You don't *sit* in a kayak, you *wear* it." To paddle effectively, you need to be snug in the cockpit with three points of contact. Your hips and lower back press squarely against the seat; your knees and upper legs connect with the inside of the upper deck under the thigh braces; and the balls of your feet push against the foot braces. Your legs should be slightly bent and spread to allow your heels to rest near the center of the kayak, while the upper part of each foot points outward and rests on the braces. If the adjustment to the foot braces is too close, you'll lose circulation in your feet. If the adjustment is too loose, your legs will straighten, reducing the support for your lower back and the control you have over your kayak.

Paddle-Brace Entry/Exit

This simple technique (Figure 4) will provide you with a stable base while getting in and out of the kayak on calm beaches. Set the boat in shallow water parallel to the beach. On the shore side of the boat, face the bow, squat next to the cockpit, and lay your paddle behind you across the deck. The paddle shaft should be perpendicular to the line of the boat, touching the outer edge of the coaming. The blade on the shore side should rest on a flat and secure surface. Reach behind and grab the shaft with your shore-side hand, while firmly grabbing the coaming and paddle shaft with your water-side hand. Shift your weight evenly to both hands and step into the boat by first sitting on the back section of the coaming, then carefully sliding your feet forward to the foot braces and your butt into the seat.

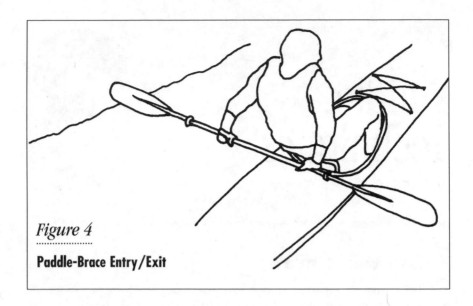

Figure 4

Paddle-Brace Entry/Exit

Dock or Pool Entry/Exit

The paddle-brace entry is also suitable for docks, floats, pool edges, and other platforms that are no higher than your boat's coaming. You use essentially the same sequence of movements as for the beach entry, except instead of squatting next to the boat, you begin by sitting along the edge of the platform with your feet forward (Figure 5).

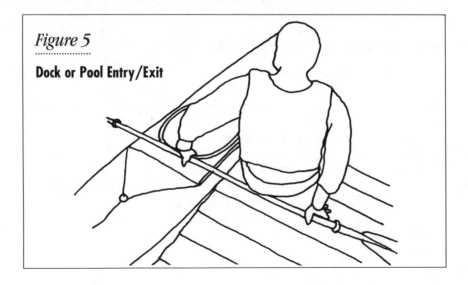

Figure 5

Dock or Pool Entry/Exit

Attaching Your Spray Skirt

A properly fitting spray skirt should be snug yet still easy to remove. Attach the skirt by first reaching behind you and securing the back of the skirt across the cockpit and around to your hips before you attach the front. Make certain that the *grab loop*—that loop of webbing attached to the front of your skirt—is sticking out: This is your "rip cord," and you'll want easy access to it in case of a capsize (see Wet Exit in Chapter 4). Finish sealing your skirt, making sure the sides are secure around the coaming. If the skirt pops off in back when you attach the front, it will actually be easier if you start over from scratch, making sure the back is on completely before reattaching the front.

Forward Stroke

Hold the paddle loosely, with your hands comfortably spaced at just beyond shoulder width. Sit with a straight back and brace with your knees and your feet. Center your balance in your hips and let your lower body sense the motion of the boat while you use torso rotation—involving the muscles of your back, shoulders, and abdomen, not just your arms—to power the stroke. To begin your stroke with the left blade, rotate your left shoulder forward while almost straightening your left arm, but do not bend forward. Reach forward with the paddle and plant the blade into the water as far forward and close to the hull of the boat as possible (Figure 6-A). Grip the paddle loosely and pull with your lower (left) hand while focusing on rotating your torso and pushing with your upper (right) hand. Keep your hands below eye level and keep your wrists straight. (Your hand should extend in line with your forearm, not be cocked up or down; Figure 6-B). Just as the left blade draws even with your hips, lift it cleanly, avoiding the common mistakes of letting it travel behind you or letting it scoop water. Then begin the second half of the cycle by rotating forward with the right blade (Figure 6-C).

A higher, more vertical stroke will be more powerful for short sprints, while a lower stroke will be easier to maintain over distance.

Reverse Stroke

To initiate a stop or to back up, use the back of the blade (don't turn the paddle around) and reach behind you, pushing forward with your lower hand. To get more power and to see where you're going, turn your body so that you're looking backward and reach back as far as you can; then use powerful back muscles to rotate your torso forward as you push the blade toward the bow.

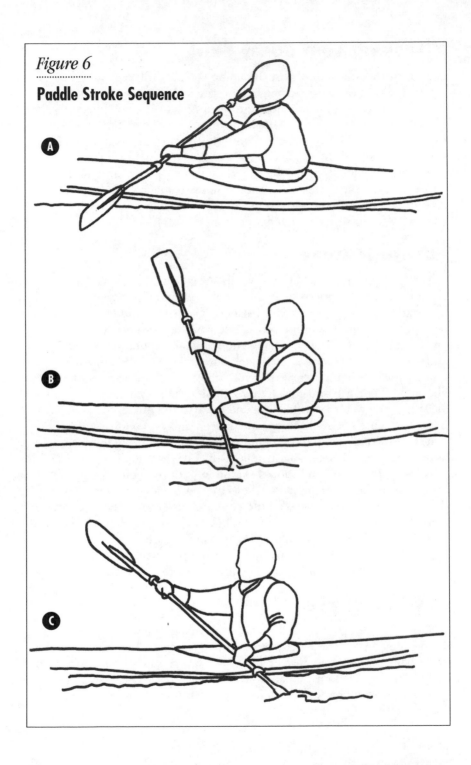

Figure 6

Paddle Stroke Sequence

Forward Sweep Stroke

To make a correction in your course while under way or to turn the boat when maneuvering in close quarters, use a *sweep stroke* (Figure 7).

Begin as you would for a forward stroke on the side opposite the direction you want to turn. Using torso rotation to push forward with your upper hand, sweep the paddle low across the deck. Keep the shaft as horizontal as possible, and still fully submerge the blade while your lower hand pulls the blade in a wide, shallow arc of nearly 180 degrees from bow to stern. A strong finish is critical to this stroke's efficiency: Turning your head and watching the blade approach the stern increases the power of the stroke by enhancing torso rotation.

Reverse Sweep Stroke and Spin Turns

A *reverse sweep* is often used in situations that demand a tight turn. It begins on the side toward which you want to turn your bow. Reaching as far behind you as possible, push the shaft with your lower hand, driving the paddle blade forward nearly 180 degrees to the bow. Just as with the forward sweep, use torso rotation to make a wide, shallow arc, keeping the paddle as horizontal as possible and submerging the blade just below the surface of the water. To turn your kayak around quickly in place, use a

Figure 7

Forward Sweep Stroke

Figure 8

Draw Stroke

spin turn—alternate the reverse sweep stroke on one side with a forward sweep stroke on the other.

Draw Stroke

The *draw stroke* (Figure 8) moves you sideways. Twist and face the side in the direction that you want to move and extend the paddle out as far as you comfortably can while still holding it in a near-vertical position. Plant the blade, face toward you, in the water (parallel to your boat) at your hips and draw the boat to the paddle. As your boat approaches the blade, be careful not to let the boat overtake the submerged paddle blade and be ready to let go with your top hand if you start to trip over your paddle.

Reset the paddle for the next stroke by rotating the blade ninety degrees (perpendicular to your boat), then slice the top edge of the blade through the water, returning it to the start position.

Bracing

Bracing is one of the most important basic paddling skills. A brace will help you avoid a capsize and maintain stability in a variety of conditions. Bracing should be a reflexive extension of your paddle stroke. If you find yourself in choppy conditions, you will be more stable if you relax your hips and continue paddling than if you stiffen up and hold the paddle out of the water as if to keep it dry, which is a common initial reaction to rough water. If you feel any instability at the beginning of your forward stroke, be prepared to perform a high brace; if you feel tippy toward the end of the stroke, try a low brace.

Low Brace

Interrupt your stroke and quickly move the paddle across your lap—centered in front of you, level with the water and perpendicular to the boat—just above deck height. With your elbows over your hands, punch straight down, slapping the back of the blade flat against the surface of the water on the side toward which you're tipping. Using the momentary

Figure 9

Low Brace

Smack the water with a straight downward motion for maximum support, elbows still up over your nearly horizontal paddle.

surface tension the water provides, push off your paddle to perform a *hip snap:* Rock the kayak squarely back beneath you with a crisp side-to-side movement of your hips and knees against the inside of your cockpit. As you recover, and downward force is no longer exerted on the now submerged blade, quickly rotate it ninety degrees to pull the top edge cleanly from the water.

High Brace

From your paddle stroke quickly bring the paddle across your cockpit about chest high, hands over elbows and in front of shoulders. (To prevent shoulder injury, it's important to keep your hands below shoulder level and in front of you.) This will bring the face of the blade on the bracing side into a position parallel with the surface of the water. (Unlike the low brace, the high brace uses the face of the blade.) Slap the water while keeping the paddle as horizontal as possible. As you would for a low brace, use a *hip snap* to bring the kayak back underneath you. Then cleanly recover the paddle by rotating it and slicing the top edge upward out of the water.

Figure 10

High Brace

Keeping the paddle as horizontal as possible, slap the water with a flat blade.

Safety

S ea-kayaking safety is an individual matter that affects the safety of the entire party. All paddlers must take responsibility for their own well-being, assessing the risk involved in any action and deciding if it's acceptable.

To properly appraise risk, a paddler must be able to perceive and evaluate the given situation. This puts the novice paddler at a disadvantage—without experience you cannot make a prudent judgment. *Act conservatively until you've gained experience and your skills are well established.*

1. Know your limits. Be honest with yourself and your companions about your experience and skill level. Stay out of any situation beyond your capabilities unless it's a controlled learning situation with experienced paddlers at hand. Don't attempt open crossings until you've mastered capsize prevention and recovery techniques. Don't paddle alone. Don't paddle in water that might get rougher than you've practiced rescues in.

2. Communicate with your companions. Never hesitate to speak up if you feel uncomfortable with a planned route or if you feel developing conditions are beyond your skills.

3. Develop your paddling skills. Braces should be repeated until they are a matter of reflex. Rescue skills should be practiced, practiced, practiced—under safe, but difficult, real-water conditions.

4. Plan your trip. Carefully plan your route, including landing sites and potential emergency pullouts, before you leave the beach.

5. Practice proper group organization. Realistically appraise the skill level of the paddlers in your group. Base decisions on the skills of the weakest paddler. Keep group sizes small—no more

than eight or ten paddlers. Use the buddy system, and keep all paddlers within earshot.

6. Be properly outfitted. All members of your paddling party should be properly outfitted. That means that each paddler should:
   - Wear a PFD
   - Carry rescue, emergency, and navigation equipment
   - Have adequate buoyancy in both bow and stern
   - Be properly clothed and have extra clothing handy

7. Know the paddling environment. Anticipate and avoid dangerous situations. Be aware of weather, winds, tides, currents, and coastal hazards.

Hypothermia

This deadly condition, caused by the lowering of your body's core temperature to below ninety-five degrees, is responsible for more sea-kayaking deaths than anything else. In fact, many fatalities attributed to drowning are the direct result of hypothermia.

Hypothermia sometimes happens slowly, the result of gradual heat loss over an extended period of time. This commonly occurs in cold, wet, and windy weather where the victim is inadequately clothed and often unaware of his worsening condition.

In a capsize, however, hypothermia can occur with alarming rapidity due to water's great ability to conduct heat. A victim in water will lose heat at a rate more than twenty times faster than in air of the same temperature. Many paddlers mistakenly assume that hypothermia is a risk only in frigidly cold conditions; it can occur in water as warm as seventy degrees, though. Hypothermia can be prevented if adequate precautions are taken: Clothing should insulate when wet. Rainwear and extra clothing should be easily accessible from the cockpit. A wet suit, dry suit, and neoprene hood or cap should be worn when there is a risk of a capsize or when practicing recoveries.

Diagnosing and Treating Hypothermia

The symptoms of hypothermia are inconsistent and unpredictable. One of its effects is a loss of mental ability—you, several of your companions, or your entire party may become hypothermic and not be aware of it. Without adequate outward signs to alert members of a paddling party, the first indication of a chronically hypothermic paddler may be a capsize.

Chronic hypothermia is indicated if a paddler begins to exhibit confused, erratic, inattentive, or sluggish behavior; slurred speech; or shivering. Hypothermia should be assumed, whether symptoms are exhibited or not, following a capsize in cold water (fifty-five degrees or lower) when the victim is not wearing a wet suit or dry suit or when there has been prolonged exposure.

To treat hypothermia:

1. Get the victim to shore as quickly as possible.
2. Handle the victim gently.
3. Remove wet clothing and replace with dry clothing or other dry covering.
4. Shelter the victim from wind and rain.
5. Insulate with a dry sleeping bag, parkas, or any other suitable material. Add moderate heat to head, neck, chest, and groin.
6. Provide something to drink. Do not give coffee or alcohol.
7. Place the victim by a fire or other heat source.
8. In severe cases seek medical attention immediately.

Recoveries and Reentries

Because hypothermia is statistically a sea kayaker's number one hazard, the ability to recover quickly from a capsize is one of the most important skills to master. Rescue skills often referred to as *recoveries* and *reentries* are best learned through hands-on experience with the supervision and support of an experienced teacher. Once learned, these are skills that all sea kayakers, novice and expert alike, must frequently practice. Pool practice is limited in its applicability to real situations—you'll rarely need to recover from a capsize in warm, calm water.

Once you have worked out the kinks in calm water, the best rough-water practice sites are locations that will provide real conditions but also have an onshore wind blowing you back toward a protected beach or calm water. Care must be taken to ensure that the practice remains a practice, not a rescue. *Good sense, good planning, and adequate support are necessities.*

Wet Exit

Before you practice getting back into your kayak, practice getting out of it. The term *wet exit* refers to the method of pushing out of your upturned kayak while underwater. Many people find this unnerving at first but quickly get comfortable with it after practicing once or twice. While you might be able to just kick your way out of your cockpit with loosely fitting spray skirts, the following technique works better with snug skirts.

Practice removing your spray skirt several times on land first. Close your eyes and hold your breath to simulate being underwater. Reach down to your hips and lean forward as you slide your hands along the coaming (this helps you locate the grab loop when you're upside down underwater and can't see). Grasp the grab loop firmly, punch forward to release the spray skirt from the lip of the coaming, and pull it off. Then run your thumbs back along the coaming to your hips to make sure the skirt is off in back. Once you're comfortable with this, it's time to try it in the water. If you're anxious, have a friend wade out into waist-deep water and stand next to you for moral support.

Take a big breath, hold it, and tip yourself over, exhaling slowly and gently through your nose to keep water out of it. Most important, try to relax while under the kayak—it takes most people only two or three seconds to resurface. Now go through the same motions as before to release the skirt; then put a hand on either side of the cockpit, tuck forward, and push it away from your hips as if you were sliding out of a tight pair of jeans. Float to the surface, take a big breath, and quickly grab your kayak and paddle. Even in light winds the kayak can blow away faster than you can swim. Eventually you will be able to wet exit without letting go of either your paddle or kayak.

T Recovery

The *T recovery* is widely considered one of the fastest, easiest, most efficient ways to get a capsized paddler back into the kayak in a variety of conditions. Because the rescuer first lifts the bow of the capsized boat to dump the water out, the swimmer reenters a kayak that is essentially dry and ready to paddle. The few extra seconds it takes to dump the water from the boat saves the several minutes it can take to pump it dry with a bilge pump.

To assist someone using this method, grab the bow of the capsized kayak and maneuver your boat perpendicular to it into the T shape from which this recovery gets its name. The swimmer then moves hand over hand to the stern of the capsized kayak, being careful to maintain constant contact with both his boat and his paddle throughout the entire

Figure 11

T recovery

maneuver. (This way, if you were to capsize during the recovery, he would still have the gear necessary to get himself back in his kayak using the *paddlefloat reentry* described later.) Have the swimmer push down on the stern of his overturned kayak at the same time you lift its bow, allowing you to pull it out of the water more easily (Figure 11-A). Generally, if you drag the bow across your lap until you can reach the front of the coaming, most of the water will quickly drain out of kayaks with rear bulkheads. (On boats without bulkheads continue pulling until the upturned kayak's cockpit is directly over your lap, then rock it back and forth like a teeter-totter until the water is drained out of each end. This version is known as the *TX recovery.*)

After draining the kayak slide it back into the water and position it alongside your own craft but facing in the opposite direction, so you can stabilize it from the front deck where you won't be in the way when the swimmer climbs onto the back deck. The swimmer then moves carefully to his cockpit on the side opposite from you and hands you his paddle. Take both paddles and place them across the fronts of both cockpits, forming a paddle bridge. Reach over the top of the paddles with both arms and lean heavily onto the other kayak to stabilize it. Grasp the empty kayak's cockpit firmly with one hand on either side of the opening and hold it steady. The swimmer faces his kayak behind the cockpit with his legs kicking out behind him on the surface of the water and uses a vigorous scissors kick to pull himself up onto the back deck (Figure 11-B). Staying on his stomach and putting an arm onto your kayak for additional support, the swimmer swings his legs into the cockpit. He then corkscrews toward the rescue boat and into a sitting position (Figure 11-C). Keep stabilizing the swimmer's boat until his spray skirt is reattached and he is ready to paddle.

Side-by-Side Reentry

This is essentially the second half of the T recovery described above. The rescuer paddles alongside and stabilizes the swimmer's kayak without first lifting its bow to drain the water. This recovery can be used in conditions where lifting the bow may be difficult or impractical—with heavily loaded boats, for example, and rough seas. Once the swimmer has reentered the swamped kayak, however, it will be necessary to take the time to remove the water with a bilge pump before paddling. This can be accomplished more quickly if both rescuer and swimmer, and perhaps a third group member if available, use their pumps at the same time.

Paddlefloat Reentry

Although assisted recoveries are generally much faster and easier, it's important to practice solo reentries, too, in case whatever capsizes you also dumps your partner. One of the best all-around self-rescues requires a piece of gear called a *paddlefloat,* which is basically an inflatable bag that slips over one end of your paddle and forms an outrigger to stabilize your waterlogged kayak. There are several features to look for in a paddlefloat: Those with dual chambers can still be used if one side fails; those that can be secured to the paddle with sturdy, plastic hardware are less likely to be kicked off the paddle during a recovery than those that rely on air pressure alone, and they are more reliable than floats with metal hardware, which can corrode or jam with sand; those with more volume will provide more flotation; and those with large valves will inflate faster. Designs made of closed-cell foam do not require inflating and may be slightly faster to deploy, but they're bulkier to store than inflatables and may offer less flotation. Store your paddlefloat in an easily reached place behind your seat or on your deck. Be sure to attach it somehow, or it may drift away when you capsize.

To perform a paddlefloat reentry, it's extremely important that you hang on to your boat while locating and setting up your paddlefloat, because it takes only a little wind to blow your boat away from you faster than you can swim. If you leave your kayak upside down on the water and hang on to it by sliding one foot into the cockpit toward the bow, both hands will be free to put the paddlefloat onto the paddle.

Start by pulling out your paddlefloat and inserting the paddle blade. Then secure the float to your paddle and inflate it. Right the kayak and set the paddle behind the cockpit perpendicular to the kayak, with the paddlefloat resting on the surface of the water. Orient yourself to face the back deck just behind the cockpit. Firmly grasp the shaft against the cockpit coaming with the hand nearest the cockpit (your right hand in this example), and kick your feet up and out behind you so that you're floating horizontally on the surface of the water. Give a vigorous scissors kick as you pull the kayak underneath you and quickly hook your (right) ankle onto the paddlefloat (Figure 12-A). Pull and push the kayak under your torso until your belly button is on its centerline.

Once you're balanced on your boat, it's important that you *keep one limb on the paddlefloat* and lean some weight onto it *throughout the entire reentry*. Put your second ankle (left) onto the paddlefloat and move the first leg (right) into the cockpit, staying on your belly with your weight held as low as possible (Figure 12-B). Be careful to keep the paddle perpendicular; don't let it scissor toward the kayak.

Figure 12

Paddlefloat reentry

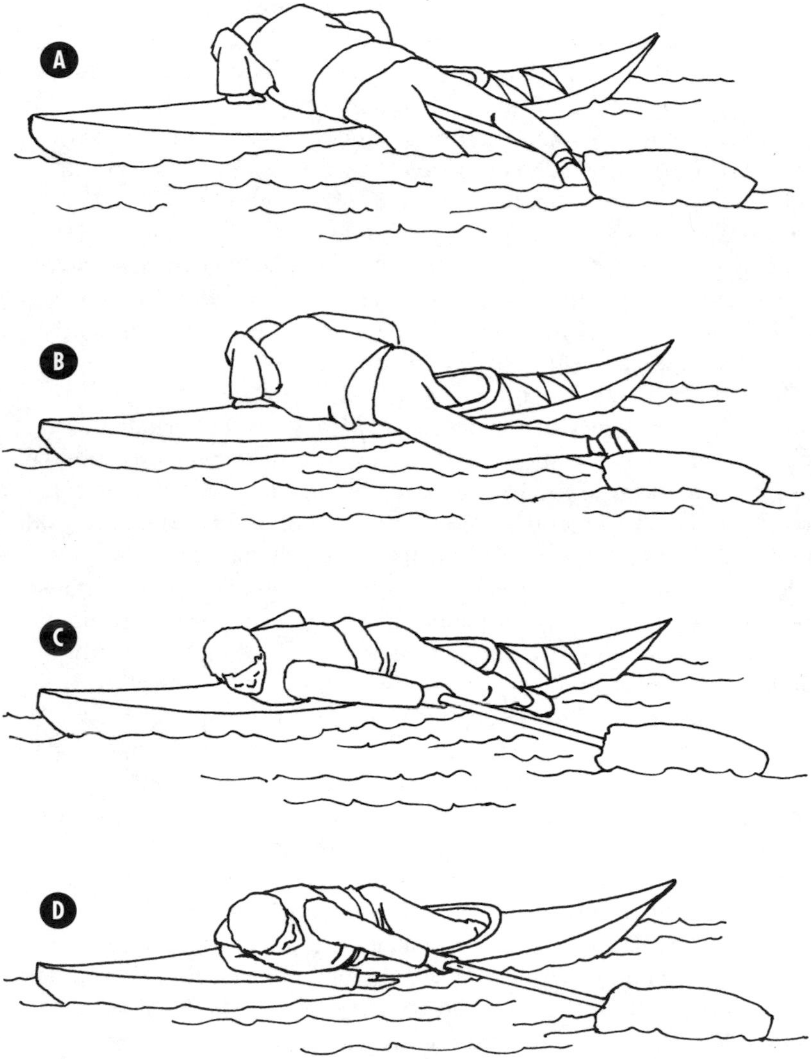

A

B

C

D

Before taking your foot (left) off the paddlefloat, you'll need to put a hand (left) onto it (Figure 12-C). This is usually the most difficult move of this reentry, because it can be a long reach. To make this easier, rotate on your belly, bringing your head across the kayak and over the water onto the paddlefloat side, then slide your hips toward the cockpit before reaching out with one hand (left) to grasp the middle of the paddle shaft. Once balanced on your hand, move the second leg into the cockpit (Figure 12-D). *Remember to continue leaning on the paddle* as you corkscrew toward the paddlefloat into the sitting position, keeping your weight on the paddlefloat side of the kayak by switching hands (left for right) on the shaft of the paddle.

Once you're in your cockpit, find your foot braces and your balance. Then bring the paddle quickly up over your head and press it against your stomach with your elbows; this way you can continue to lean on it for support while you grab your bilge pump and begin pumping your kayak out. If rough seas are causing waves to slosh into your kayak, you may need to replace your spray skirt, leaving a small opening on the side away from the waves for your pump. Don't bother trying to pump your boat completely dry. You can stop when the pump starts to sputter because it's sucking a lot of air and you have less than an inch of water left in your boat. Replace your pump, then remove your paddlefloat and deflate it, remembering to close the nozzle before stowing it so the bladder doesn't take on water.

Other Recoveries or Reentries

There are dozens of reentry techniques, as well as several variations on those described above. But the standard paddlefloat reentry and T recovery are two good bread-and-butter techniques, because they're simple and effective. Once you've mastered these two, it's recommended that you broaden your repertoire to include as many as possible. Learning more recoveries increases your options in case of an unexpected capsize. Some techniques involve using a loop of line known as a sling that acts as a stirrup to help a tired paddler climb up onto her boat. Other methods allow you to recover from a capsize without even executing a wet exit. In the kayak roll, for instance, the inverted paddler uses his paddle to right his own kayak; in the bow recovery, you as the rescuer offer your kayak bow to the inverted paddler, who grabs it to right her craft. Educate yourself through classes and clinics on the water, and you'll be much safer while paddling.

Towing

A towline comes in handy for recovering kayaks that have escaped people during recoveries, for helping someone who is injured or seasick, or for just lending a little forward momentum to a weary paddler. A line of about 15 feet is necessary for flat water; 25 to 30 feet works better in rougher water or following seas (see Chapter 5). Longer lines are unnecessary, because they can be difficult to manage and time consuming to stow. The attachment to the kayak under tow can be by clip, carabiner, or simple knot. The attachment to the rescuer should be quick release. Some people prefer towbelts that secure around their waists; others use towing systems incorporated into their PFDs or jam cleats added to their rear decks. In any method the attachment needs to be close to the center of the kayak and able to be secured or removed quickly. Towing is easiest if the towed boat can stay in line with the towing kayak without excessive yawing; rudders may help. Practice attaching, deploying, and towing before you really need these skills.

On the Water

When you place your boat on the water, you enter a changing world of tides, currents, wind, and waves. Every sea kayaker should become well acquainted with the watery environment where he paddles. This chapter introduces basic considerations to prepare for protected-water paddling: wind and weather, tides and currents, launching and landing through small surf, basic navigation, and trip planning.

Wind and Weather

Considering the strength and direction of the wind is extremely important when planning a trip. A headwind of as little as 10 or 15 knots can slow your forward progress to a crawl, tire you out, or even blow you off course into potentially hazardous conditions. Even a tailwind can create difficult or dangerous paddling conditions. The longer and stronger the wind blows across open water, regardless of direction, the rougher the water will become. Waves will form, and choppy seas can capsize a paddler and make self-rescue difficult. Remember that at around 10 knots, whitecaps will begin forming on the water, and these are a good indication that beginning kayakers should either stay ashore or head for shelter (if they're already on the water), unless they're well versed at rough-water recoveries.

It's a good practice to check the weather report before every trip—preferably a current marine forecast from your weather radio just prior to launching. Then plan your route to either avoid or take advantage of forecast winds. A common strategy is to paddle upwind in the morning, so the wind will be at your back on the return. By taking the time to learn about local weather patterns—prevailing wind directions, morning fog, afternoon thunderstorms—you will have a much easier, and much safer, time on the water.

Following Seas and Crosswinds

When the wind is at your back, it helps push you along toward your destination. But tailwinds can also create some of the most challenging conditions to paddle in, especially if waves begin to form, becoming what mariners refer to as *following seas.* Controlling the steering and stability of your kayak can grow difficult, because the wind and seas tend to turn the boat sideways. *Crosswinds*—those that blow across your direction of travel—can also be challenging. Your stern will be more easily pushed downwind than the bow, so you'll feel like your kayak is constantly turning upwind like a weather vane. In fact, this effect is referred to as *weather-cocking* or *weather-vaning.*

In either condition maintain your course with sweep strokes or your rudder. If your kayak doesn't have a rudder, you can use your paddle like one. Place the paddle blade into the water at an angle behind you as if you were starting a reverse sweep (see Chapter 3). This will cause your kayak to lose momentum on that side, slowing and turning toward the side that the paddle is on. If the seas are steep, relax your torso, letting your hips ride the irregularities of the water surface, and prepare to brace on the upwind side.

Tides and Currents

Tides

Tides are a gravitational effect of the sun and moon. The moon, though it is considerably smaller than the sun, has a greater effect because it is much closer. Its gravitational pull creates a bulge of water that circles the earth every twenty-four hours and fifty minutes or so. High and low areas in the bulge, in conjunction with numerous smaller factors, account for the daily rise and fall of the tides. Depending on location, most areas have *semidiurnal tides*—two high tides alternating with two lows every six hours or so—while some areas have *diurnal tides,* which consist of one high and one low tide approximately twelve hours apart.

Tide height is the up-and-down motion of water drawn toward the moon. The average of the lower low tides—called *mean low water*—at a particular reference point is indicated as 0.0 feet. The vertical distance between the highest and lowest tides can range from only a foot or two in the tropics to more than 40 feet at higher latitudes.

Tides create a constantly changing topography as the waters alternately cover and expose the shore. A suitable landing site that lies within yards of a campsite at high tide, for instance, might require a long hike across an exposed mudflat at low tide. Consult a tide chart before paddling in tidally influenced waters, giving careful consideration to all decisions regarding landing and campsites.

Currents

As the water cycles through the up-and-down motion of the tides, it also moves in and out—these are the *tidal currents.* A tidal current flowing into a coastal embayment is called the *flood;* when it moves out it's called the *ebb.* The period between ebb and flood, when there is little or no movement of the water, is called *slack water.* The strength of a current is dependent on the size of the tide—the volume of water being moved—and the shape of the landform through which the water must move. As the current cycles from slack to ebb or flood, it builds to a maximum speed, known as *maximum ebb* or *maximum flood.*

Currents can be both a help and a hazard for paddlers. The hydraulics created by water moving rapidly through narrow passages can be very dangerous, and the steep waves formed by winds moving against the direction of the current's flow can be a hazard. Both situations should be approached at slack water for those without well-developed bracing and rough-water recovery skills. Be especially aware of outgoing (ebb) currents near narrow mouths—of rivers, estuaries, or lagoons—where strong currents may sweep you out to sea; several kayaking fatalities have occurred this way. On the other hand, currents can be a great help when you plan your route through safe waters with the direction of the flow. Current tables and charts should be used to predict the time, direction, and volume of flow for any given area.

If you do find yourself moving against the current, position your kayak close to shore where the flow of water is the weakest. As a general rule, rising tides with incoming (flood) currents will be safer, because you won't get stuck in the mud or swept out to sea as you might on an ebb.

Crossing a Current

Maintaining a specific course when you're crossing a current is not a consideration if your destination is simply the opposite shore of a long channel or a point well downstream of where you begin your crossing. In fact, if you want to make the quickest possible crossing to the opposite shore, in order to outrun weather or limit your exposure in the open water of the channel, your best choice is to simply paddle straight across and let the current move you downstream.

Maintaining your course when crossing becomes important if you must reach a specific point directly across on the opposite shore. If you simply launch and attempt to paddle directly to your destination, you'll be swept sideways and away from your intended landing by the flow of water.

The technique used for the controlled crossing of a current is *ferrying*—angling your boat into the current so that you move from shore to shore along a predictable line. As you ferry across the channel, you'll be paddling into the current and moving at a speed that is less than your actual paddling speed. You control the line of your crossing by orienting the angle of your forward direction and your paddling speed to compensate for the direction and speed of the water. Your paddling speed and the speed of the current will determine the correct angle. This is known as the *ferry angle*.

The simplest way to set the ferry angle and maintain a course across a current is to use a natural range (Figure 13). Houses, trees, large rocks, hills, and other shoreline landmarks all make convenient targets. To establish your range, select two landmarks in line with your destination. The correct angle will be indicated by the relative positions of landmarks. Keep them in line and you're on course. Correct your speed and angle by adjusting to the positions of the landmarks. Once you've found the correct angle and speed, refer to your compass and note the heading, or check the shore for additional landmarks that will remain visible and in line as you approach your destination. Use these to maintain your course as you approach the shore.

It's wise to overcorrect at the beginning of a crossing by heading slightly upstream of your destination. The current is likely to be fastest in the deeper water at the midpoint of the channel, so a prudent beginning will allow greater room for error as your crossing proceeds.

When deciding where to cross, bear in mind that the current accelerates as a waterway narrows; thus the section of a channel with the shortest shore-to-shore span is not necessarily the best place to cross. A longer crossing through slower water may be a better choice.

You should also consider what lies downstream. Don't cross at a location where there's a chance that you'll be carried into open water, rips, or other dangerous conditions.

When to cross depends largely on your route and the speed of the current. If you're traveling well downstream of a moderate current, you can plan to cross using the current for an additional push. When traveling across the channel to a specific point, you would ideally cross at slack water when the current is at its weakest. This window of time can be determined by using tidal current tables, if they exist for that area.

Surf Launches and Landings

In some coastal areas the ability to handle small surf is essential. (Note that surf above shoulder or head height when you're sitting in your kayak is generally recommended only for intermediate or advanced paddlers

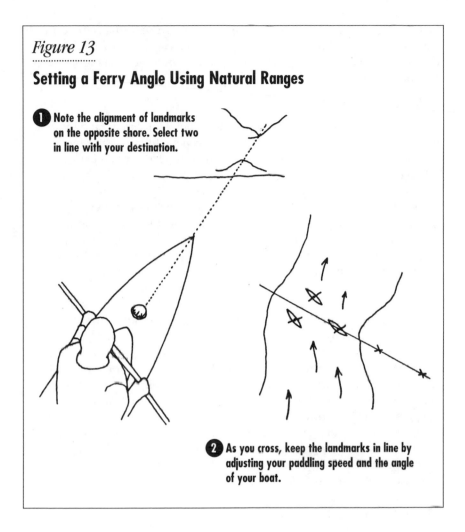

Figure 13

Setting a Ferry Angle Using Natural Ranges

1 Note the alignment of landmarks on the opposite shore. Select two in line with your destination.

2 As you cross, keep the landmarks in line by adjusting your paddling speed and the angle of your boat.

who have previous training and are wearing helmets.) Even in protected areas a good wind can raise small waves that make launching and landing difficult. It is strongly recommended that anyone expecting to encounter surf should get competent, professional training *beforehand.*

Launching

Try to pick a protected beach that's out of the direct line of incoming waves. When you're paddling with a group, the most skilled paddler should launch last after helping the others to launch one at a time. Keep your bow perpendicular to oncoming waves, and try to launch in a "window" between waves. Don't stop paddling if a wave hits you; paddle hard and try to punch through. In the case of a capsize, move quickly away from your boat, being extremely careful not to get caught between your boat and shore.

Landing

The most skilled paddler lands first, then helps others to land by grabbing their bows and stabilizing their kayaks while pulling them out of the water. Subsequent paddlers should land one at a time, and anyone helping them to land must exercise extreme caution to avoid being run into by an incoming kayak. Try to pick a window between waves, following immediately behind a wave to avoid surfing. If a breaking wave catches your stern, it will tend to broach your boat sideways and dump you toward shore. Try to counteract this by leaning into the waves and bracing a flat paddle onto the foam. If you capsize, it's much safer to fall into the wave than to get dumped onto shore.

Navigation

Kayak navigation begins with a carefully planned route. After that comes the disarmingly simple–sounding task of keeping track of where you are and where you want to go. It can be as easy as sighting various landmarks along a sunny shore and locating them on your chart, or as challenging as executing an open-water crossing well out of sight of land. This book offers a cursory look at the tools of kayak navigation for nearshore travel in protected waters. The skills and techniques needed for open-coast paddling and open-water crossings are beyond the range of any novice and beyond the scope of this book. For a more in-depth treatment of kayak navigation, read *Fundamentals of Kayak Navigation* by David Burch (see Appendix II).

Navigation Tools

Nautical Charts

Charts of U.S. waters are published by the National Ocean Survey (NOS), a department of the National Oceanographic and Atmospheric Administration (NOAA). Charts of Canadian waters are available from the Canadian Hydrographic Service. These nautical charts provide you with invaluable information about coastal features and are essential to navigation. Depth readings (soundings) are indicated numerically in feet, meters, or fathoms (6 feet); shoreline tidal range is often indicated by color; and symbols are used to indicate shoreline composition and obstructions. Navigation aids (such as buoys and lights), landforms, and other features visible from the water are also indicated by symbols.

Every beginning navigator should first acquire the pamphlet titled *Chart No. 1.* This key to the meanings of chart symbols is available at most chart dealers.

Generally, novice kayakers should use the most detailed chart for the area they will be paddling. This means the chart with the largest scale— 1:20,000 (1 inch on the chart equals 20,000 inches of the area mapped) or larger. Remember that the scale increases as the second number decreases. A 1:40,000 chart is less detailed than a 1:20,000 chart.

To locate the charts for an area you plan to visit, you'll need the NOAA Nautical Chart Catalog for the region. Consult the catalog's coverage diagram; the accompanying list will tell you the name, number, and scale of each chart shown. Each catalog also includes the addresses of authorized chart dealers in the region.

Chart Case

A clear plastic chart case with a watertight seal serves two important functions: It keeps your charts dry, and it provides a means of securing your charts to the deck, where they will be accessible without opening the spray skirt.

Tidal Current Charts and Tables

Also published by NOS, tidal current charts and tables show the direction and speed of tidal flow.

Tide Tables

Familiar to most ocean anglers, tide tables indicate the times and heights of high and low water for various reference stations within a given area.

Topographic Maps

Nautical charts provide very limited landform information. U.S. Geological Survey topographic maps are useful for selecting suitable sites for sheltering from winds, landing, and camping.

Compass

You can use either a handheld orienteering-style compass or a more expensive, but more convenient, deck-mounted marine compass.

Dividers

Small dividers are used to accurately and easily measure distances on a chart.

Straightedge and Grease Pencil

A small plastic ruler tethered to your chart case, or the edge of a handheld compass, can be used to draw bearing lines onto your chart case.

Global Positioning System

GPS use has become more common as the price of water-resistant, handheld models has dropped to near $100. The devices, which use satellite signals to locate your latitude and longitude to well within 50 feet or less, are handy for those who possess basic navigational skills but are of little use to those without the ability to read a chart or compass.

Piloting

Every kayaking trip begins from a known point. As you move from that point, you must keep track of your position. This can most easily be accomplished by *piloting*—a method of navigation familiar to any of you who've found your way through an unfamiliar city by using recognizable landmarks.

To navigate by piloting on water, you simply note landmarks on the shore (lights, headlands, and so forth) or on the water (buoys and other navigational aids). Next, locate the landmark on the chart and identify your position on the water relative to the landmark.

A more precise means of noting your location is by using a *range*—a line through two fixed points. If you draw a line along the headlands of two small islands (Figure 14), you know that at the moment the closer island obscures the more distant island, you're located along that line. This is called a *line of position.* An intersecting line drawn from another range or a compass reading off another landmark will indicate or *fix* your approximate location.

To take the compass reading, aim the compass at the target. If you're using a deck-mounted compass, point the bow toward the target. Keep as steady as possible until an average reading can be established. This is your *bearing.* Draw a line along that bearing extending out from the target. If no ranges are available, two compass bearing lines can be used to fix your position.

Trip Planning

Planning is essential to every kayak trip—even a lunch-hour outing. You must determine how much time you have for the trip, the distance to be traveled, and how long it will take. A safe route must be selected.

Figure 14

Taking a Range

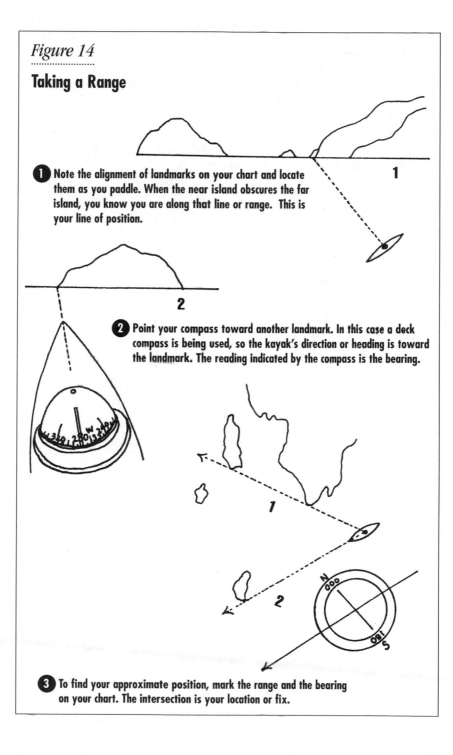

1 Note the alignment of landmarks on your chart and locate them as you paddle. When the near island obscures the far island, you know you are along that line or range. This is your line of position.

2 Point your compass toward another landmark. In this case a deck compass is being used, so the kayak's direction or heading is toward the landmark. The reading indicated by the compass is the bearing.

3 To find your approximate position, mark the range and the bearing on your chart. The intersection is your location or fix.

Tides, currents, winds, and weather must be taken into account. Possible landing and campsites must be considered.

A touring kayak with an average paddler will move at a comfortable cruising speed of between 2 or 3 knots. For an enjoyable day trip, plan nothing more than three to four hours of paddling time, about 8 nautical miles round-trip. When figuring distances and times for longer trips, accounting for stops, weather, rest days, and other delays, plan on a conservative average of about 8 nautical miles per day. By that standard a seven-day trip could comfortably cover 56 miles.

Packing and Loading

For many paddlers one of the best things about sea kayaks is their ability to transport you and a bunch of your gear to beautiful and remote shores. A typical touring kayak can easily hold two backpacks worth of food and camping gear, and you don't have to carry it on your back! But how you pack and load your gear is more than a matter of convenience—it will affect the safety of your journey and the seaworthiness of your boat. Important items such as extra clothing and emergency equipment must be easily accessible. Waterproof bags must be used to protect your gear from the damaging effects of water and to provide flotation in case of a capsize. And finally, your gear must be well secured and distributed so that your boat will maintain proper balance.

Packing Your Gear

Store any items that would be damaged by contact with water in durable, waterproof dry bags. These bags will not only keep your equipment dry, but they will also provide added buoyancy. Your sleeping bag and spare clothing could be critical in a survival situation and should always be well protected from water.

Do not overfill dry bags. Leave a little extra space so that the bag's material is not stretched taut. This will make the bag less prone to punctures (it will also be easier to fit in the boat). Pack your sleeping bag in its stuff sack and then slip it inside a roomy dry bag, or simply pack it directly into a dry bag.

It's easier and safer to use a number of smaller bags than several large ones. The smaller bags allow for more efficient use of the boat's storage space, and their greater numbers mean your gear will suffer less damage from a single leak.

Take particular care when you fill and close roll-down bags—usually it's not the fabric that leaks, it's the seal. Fill the bags about two-thirds full and squeeze the air out. Fold the closure so that the material is smooth, with tight, crisp turns.

Organize your gear by use, just as you would if you were packing a backpack. Items that are used together should be packed together whenever possible. Separate food into several bags divided into rations for every few days.

Loading Your Boat

Trim is a boat's bow-to-stern balance in the water. Generally it's best to adjust for level trim, but you may find that your particular boat handles more to your liking with the load slightly heavier toward the bow or stern.

For even trim and weight distribution, you'll typically end up with nearly two-thirds of your weight in the stern and one-third in the bow; since most kayaks are longer in front, they'll be bow heavy if you load equal weight fore and aft. Pack lighter, narrower objects—tent poles, sleeping pads, tarps—in the far ends of your bow and stern. Heavy items—water, fuel, food—should be placed aft, with the heaviest items along the centerline and as close to the cockpit and as low as possible. Spare warm clothes, lunch, and other items that should be easily accessible when you land can be stowed last. Smaller items that you want to reach while paddling can go in a dry bag behind your seat or even between your legs, provided the bag is not big enough to interfere with a safe wet exit if you capsize.

On Deck

The deck is the place for gear that you want access to without opening your spray skirt, or for awkward items that won't fit below. You should restrict your deck load to items that are lightweight, won't catch the wind, and won't be damaged by exposure to heat, sun, salt water, and rain.

Your chart case and compass should be securely attached just forward of the cockpit. Small items can be kept in a small deck bag. Larger items, like your spare paddle or fishing rod, should be securely tied to cleats with nylon line. Use shock cords (bungees) only to keep things snug.

Carrying an Unloaded Kayak

First, empty any water that might be inside the boat. Remove the hatches and, with the help of another person positioned at the opposite end of the boat, lift it by grabbing the bow and stern. Invert it so that the deck is facing the ground. Drain the water by first raising one end, then the other, so that the water exits from the cockpit and hatch openings.

When two people are carrying the boat, simply use the grab loops located at the stern and bow. If you're alone, and fairly strong, you can carry the boat by lifting it up and resting the inside of the coaming on your shoulder. Balance the boat by positioning your shoulder at the boat's center of gravity and steadying the load with your free hand.

Another method, useful for long hauls or if your boat is too heavy or cumbersome to carry on your shoulder, is to use a small two-wheeled cart. These carts, available at most kayak dealers, attach to the boat's stern and allow you to roll your way between the car and the put-in.

Carrying a Loaded Kayak

The best practice is to avoid carrying a kayak when it's fully loaded— it's hazardous for both you and your boat.

If you must move a loaded boat, the best method is the strap carry recommended by John Dowd, author of *Sea Kayaking: A Manual for Long Distance Touring.* You'll need two straps made of 2-inch nylon webbing 4 to 8 feet long with grab loops sewn at each end. When four people are present, run two straps under the boat, one at the bow and one at the stern about 3 feet in from the end. This safely distributes the load without placing undue stress on any single area of the hull and allows the carriers to hoist the heavy load with their legs, not their backs.

If you're alone or with one other person, use a strap to lift one end of the boat at a time, walking it up the beach by rotating it 180 degrees with each turn.

If you have no straps, you can avoid excess stress on the grab loops by reaching under the bow and stern and lifting the boat by the keel.

Getting
There

Cartopping

Many kayaks see almost as much road time as water time; you may even feel you put your kayak in the water just to wash the road grit off! Before you pull onto the highway for your first trip, here are a few things you should know.

Don't scrimp on racks. Buy a quality set that locks securely to your car. Yakima- and Thule-brand racks top the list. They're sturdy, dependable, and able to accommodate a variety of sporting equipment.

Place the racks on your car so that the crossbars are as far apart as possible. If they're too close together, the boat will be less stable and most of its weight will be concentrated on one area of the hull.

Fiberglass kayaks should be placed right-side up with the hull resting on cradles. Polyethylene kayaks are best carried upside down with the deck resting on cradles so that any deformation will not misshape the hull and affect performance. When the boat is in the water, the deck will be heated by the sun and quickly return to its original shape.

Secure your kayak to the crossbars using the cam straps (1-inch nylon webbing with metal buckles; Figure 15) available at most kayak shops. Run the strap over your kayak, around the middle of the crossbar, and then back over your boat. Position the buckle facing downward several inches above the bar, and loop the strap's other end around the bar, making sure to wrap it *inside* the rack's towers so it won't slip off. Next, run the end through the self-tightening buckle, and snug your boat to the rack with a downward pull. The straps should be tight enough that you can rock your car by pulling gently on the kayak, but not so tight that your hull or deck is visibly (or *audibly,* in the case of crunching fiberglass) compressed. Finish off by wrapping any excess strap around

B A S I C   E S S E N T I A L S

Figure 15

Securing Kayak to Rack with a Cam Strap

1 Loop the strap around the middle of the bar.

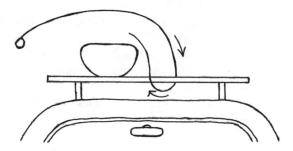

2 Leave the buckle above the bar and wrap the other end around the bar inside the tower.

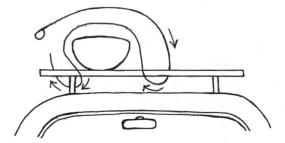

3 Pull downward on the strap to cinch down the buckle.

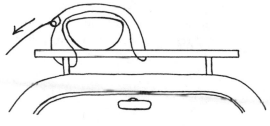

the tower and securing the end with a half hitch. Some kayakers also like to secure bow and stern lines from their grab loops to their front and rear bumpers. Make these lines snug, but be careful to avoid excess downward pressure on the ends of your boat.

Do not use elastic cords (bungees). These stretch too easily, allowing your boat to bounce and shift position. Make a habit of always tying your boat down as soon as it's placed on the rack and removing your boat as soon as it's untied. Many unsecured boats have been damaged when blown from racks by unexpected gusts of wind.

Use a security cable to discourage thieves and improve your peace of mind. Many boats are available with holes or permanently fixed metal cleats large enough to thread a cable through. If your boat doesn't have a place to attach the cable, wrap the cable tightly around the boat. In either case lock the cable ends to your rack.

Most auto insurance policies will not cover your boat if it's stolen while on your car, so schedule theft coverage for your boat through your household insurer.

In the Air

Three-quarters of our world's surface is covered with water—a heady thought when you're a paddler with an itch to travel. But distant destinations often mean flying, and that's where the trouble begins. Show up unprepared at check-in time with a load of gear and a kayak and you're looking for trouble.

No major airline has a specific policy regarding accepting kayaks as either checked baggage or freight. Most carriers will allow kayaks as freight on a space-available basis. Unfortunately, air freight is very expensive; the cost of shipping a boat will often exceed the price of your own ticket.

If you plan to fly often, consider an inflatable or breakdown boat. Most airlines will accept them without question as checked baggage.

Pack your gear neatly. A jumble of gear bags with dangling straps increases your chances of losing equipment, infuriating baggage handlers, and alienating check-in personnel. Every bag should be clearly marked, inside and out, with your name and destination. To protect your home while you're away, only the inside tag should have your home address.

Appendix I

GLOSSARY

Aft: Toward the stern from the cockpit.

Beam: The widest part of the kayak.

Bearing: The compass direction to a landmark.

Blade: The flat part of a paddle.

Bow: The front end of the kayak.

Bulkhead: A waterproof wall dividing sections of a kayak's interior.

Centerline: An imaginary line running lengthwise, dividing the kayak into equal left and right halves.

Coaming: The lip that surrounds the cockpit where the spray skirt attaches.

Cockpit: The opening in the kayak's deck where the paddler sits.

Course: The direction you want to go.

Deck: The top half of the kayak.

Dry Bag: Waterproof bags used to store gear.

Dry Suit: A waterproof garment with watertight seals at the neck, wrist, and ankles.

Face: The portion of the paddle blade designed to push against the water.

Feathered: Paddle blades rotated off the same plane on the axis of the paddle shaft.

Float Bags: Contoured nylon or plastic inflatable bags that fit into the boat's bow and stern.

Forward: Toward the bow from the cockpit.

Gel-Coat: The abrasion-resistant outer layer in a molded fiberglass-and-resin kayak.

GPS (Global Positioning System): Navigational devices that use satellite signals to locate your latitude and longitude to within 50 feet.

Heading: The direction the kayak is pointed.

Hull: The bottom half of a kayak.

Life Vest: See PFD.

Line of Position: A range on which you are located.

Painters: Lines at the bow and stern of the kayak.

PFD (Personal Flotation Device): A foam-filled vest worn for flotation.

Range: A line on a chart extended from a straight road or shoreline, or from the alignment of two landmarks.

Shaft: The round tube connecting the paddle blades.

Spray Skirt: Water-resistant seal between the paddler and the kayak's coaming.

Stern: The back end of a kayak.

Trim: The bow-to-stern balance of the kayak.

Wet Suit: Garment that insulates by trapping water next to the skin beneath a layer of closed-cell neoprene foam.

Appendix II

SUGGESTED READING

BOOKS

Bascom, Willard. *Waves and Beaches.* New York: Anchor Books, 1980.

Broze, Matt, and George Gronseth. *Sea Kayaker's Deep Trouble: True Stories and Their Lessons from Sea Kayaker Magazine.* New York: McGraw-Hill, 1997.

Burch, David. *Fundamentals of Kayak Navigation.* Guilford, CT: The Globe Pequot Press, 1999.

Dowd, John. *Sea Kayaking: A Manual for Long Distance Touring.* Seattle, WA: University of Washington Press, 1988.

Forgey, William, M.D. *The Basic Essentials of Hypothermia.* Guilford, CT: The Globe Pequot Press, 1999.

Foster, Nigel. *Nigel Foster's Surf Kayaking.* Guilford, CT: The Globe Pequot Press, 1998.

Hutchinson, Derek. *Derek C. Hutchinson's Sea Kayaking Basics.* Guilford, CT: The Globe Pequot Press, 1999.

Johnson, Shelly. *Sea Kayaking: A Woman's Guide.* Blacklick, OH: International Marine/Ragged Mountain Press, 1998.

Robison, John. *Sea Kayaking Illustrated: A Visual Guide to Better Paddling.* Blacklick, OH: International Marine/Ragged Mountain Press, 2003.

Schumann, Roger et al. *Sea Kayak Rescue: The Definitive Guide to Modern Reentry and Recovery Techniques.* Guilford CT: The Globe Pequot Press, 2001.

Sutherland, Audrey. *Paddling Hawaii: An Insider's Guide to Exploring the Secluded Coves, Jungle Streams, and Wild Coasts of the Hawaiian Islands.* Seattle, WA: The Mountaineers, 1988.

Washburne, Randal. *Coastal Kayaker's Manual: A Complete Guide to Skills, Gear, and Sea Sense.* Guilford, CT: The Globe Pequot Press, 1998.

PERIODICALS

Canoe and Kayak: Covers a broad spectrum of paddling subjects, including sea kayaking. Published six times a year, including an annual buyer's guide with complete listings of boats and accessories. P.O. Box 3146, Kirkland, WA 98083; www.canoekayak.com.

Paddler: Covers a broad spectrum of paddling subjects, including sea kayaking. Published six times a year. P.O. Box 775450, Steamboat Springs, CO 80477; www.aca-paddler.org/paddler.

Sea Kayaker: An information-packed resource. Published six times a year. 7001 Seaview Avenue Northwest, Suite 135, Seattle, WA 98117; www.seakayakermag.com.

Appendix III

EQUIPMENT CHECKLIST

DAY TRIP

- ❑ Kayak
- ❑ PFD
- ❑ Dry bags
- ❑ Emergency signal kit
- ❑ Pump
- ❑ Chart and case
- ❑ Tide tables
- ❑ Wind shell
- ❑ Pogies
- ❑ Sunglasses
- ❑ Flashlight
- ❑ Matches/lighter
- ❑ Small vice-grip pliers
- ❑ Towel
- ❑ Toilet paper
- ❑ Pee bottle

- ❑ Paddle
- ❑ Spray skirt
- ❑ Recovery gear
- ❑ Weather radio
- ❑ Sponge
- ❑ Compass
- ❑ Current chart
- ❑ Pile jacket
- ❑ Footwear
- ❑ Wet suit
- ❑ Sunscreen
- ❑ Duct tape
- ❑ Tarp
- ❑ Emergency blanket
- ❑ Trowel
- ❑ Recovery gear

- ❑ Spare paddle
- ❑ Buoyancy bags
- ❑ Whistle/air horn
- ❑ Binoculars
- ❑ Towline
- ❑ Wristwatch
- ❑ Rainwear
- ❑ Change of clothes
- ❑ Sun hat
- ❑ Water bottle
- ❑ Insect repellent
- ❑ Screwdriver
- ❑ Line *(100-foot parachute cord)*
- ❑ Basic first-aid kit

OVERNIGHT, ADD:

- ❑ Tent
- ❑ Cook kit
- ❑ Food
- ❑ Hatchet or saw
- ❑ Toilet kit

- ❑ Sleeping bag
- ❑ Utensils
- ❑ Fuel
- ❑ Extra clothes
- ❑ Day pack

- ❑ Sleeping pad
- ❑ Stove
- ❑ Water bag
- ❑ Repair kit
- ❑ Spare sunglasses

Index

About the Authors

J. Michael Wyatt is a professional outdoor photographer and writer who lives in Washington State.

Roger Schumann owns and operates Eskape Sea Kayaking school, based in Santa Cruz, California. He is also the co-author of the NOBA award-winning *Guide to Sea Kayaking Central & Northern California* and *Sea Kayak Rescue.*